BLINDNESS

BLINDNESS

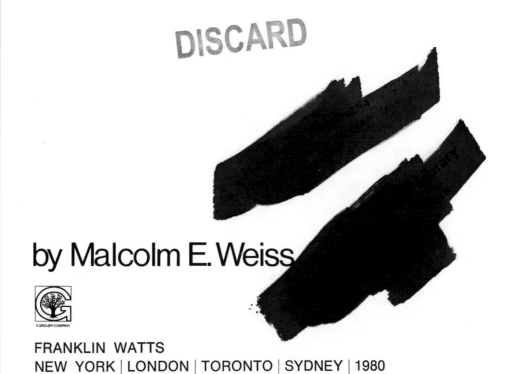

by Malcolm E. Weiss

FRANKLIN WATTS
NEW YORK | LONDON | TORONTO | SYDNEY | 1980
A FIRST BOOK

Photographs courtesy of: Irene Bayer/Monkmeyer Press Photo Service: pp. 6, 18, 29, 45; Freda Leinwand/Monkmeyer Press Photo Service: p. 32; Maurice Frink, Jr./Monkmeyer Press Photo Service: p. 34; Telesensory Systems, Inc.: p. 36; Martin L. Schneider/Associates: p. 38; Nancy Kaye/Leo de Wys, Inc.: p. 41; Westcott/Leo de Wys, Inc.: p. 50; IBM: p. 54.

Illustrations courtesy of Vantage Art, Inc.

Library of Congress Cataloging in Publication Data

Malcolm E
ness.

es blindness and how
me this handicap.
e literature. [1. Blind.
2. Physical   d]   Title.
RE91.W44   '9712   80–14059
ISBN 0–531–02939–5

Contents

BLINDNESS

Chapter 1
SARAH

The alarm didn't go off, because it was a Saturday. No school. But Sarah stirred sleepily on her bed, listening.

She remembered waking up during the night, hearing a rooster crowing far off. Then she'd gone back to sleep. It seemed like just a few minutes ago.

But it couldn't be. There were many birds singing now. They were the early spring arrivals. She could pick them out by their different calls.

The breeze blowing through her room was already warmer than it had been. Sarah threw off the covers and got up. Her slippers were lined up neatly, right next to the bed. No time for them, thought Sarah, and she hurried toward the window. The carpet felt soft and warmish against her bare feet. Near the window, the carpet ended. The floor boards were harder and cooler.

Sarah leaned out the window and turned her face toward the sun. She felt the light pour over her like a warm shower. She loved to turn toward the sun and feel it staring back at her. Every time she did, she was reminded of Dad's favorite nickname for her: Sunflower.

She wondered how sunflowers found the sun. Did they feel the sunlight somewhere in their smooth petals and fuzzy centers? Did they somehow see the sun?

Sarah didn't. She never had. Sarah had been born blind.

Like most babies, the first people Sarah learned to know were her parents. Even before she began to talk, she knew how to tell them apart. There was the difference in their voices and the feel of their faces. There were differences in the way they picked her up and held her.

All these things were part of her earliest memories. Sarah didn't know then that she was blind. Sometimes she found herself trying to think back to those early days of her life. When was it she first found out that her eyes didn't work?

She couldn't remember. Her earliest memories were in bits and pieces, with big empty spaces in between.

Once, in the attic, she'd found an old window screen. It was badly damaged by rust and wear. She had run her fingers over the screen, feeling the regular little squares of the wire mesh. There were lots of ragged holes breaking up the pattern.

Trying to remember those early days was like feeling that screen. Here and there was a memory, clear and sharp—a pattern, something that made sense. In between were the blank empty spaces, times with no memories. As she grew older, there were more memories and fewer empty places.

[2

There were bright memories of learning how to talk. Once she started she'd been eager—very eager.

Sarah thought she knew why she had been in such a hurry to talk. Mom and Dad encouraged her. They talked to her a lot. And it seemed to Sarah that the big thing had happened on a single day.

She was in a playpen. Her mother was in the kitchen. All afternoon, they talked back and forth. They talked about the toys Sarah was playing with. They talked about what her mother was doing in the kitchen. It was as if they had been together in the same room all the time. Talking was a way of being together, even at a distance.

Sarah didn't really believe things had happened all at once like that. The memory of that long afternoon was like a dream where things that might take days or years happen in a few minutes. It takes longer than an afternoon to learn the joy of words.

What was true about that memory was the pleasure of it.

But she had learned to talk step by step. And so it must have been with finding out that she was blind.

There were the bright memories of talking. Mixed in with them were other memories. Sarah called them "puzzle memories."

"Watch out, Sarah. Box!"

There were many warnings like that while Sarah was learning to talk. And each time, she wondered: How did her parents know something was in her way?

They explained patiently, over and over. It must have been hard to explain to a small girl who did not know many words, who had no idea what "seeing" meant. Sarah knew that now. But slowly, bit by bit, Sarah came to understand that she was blind.

Chapter 2
SEEING

Sarah is totally blind. In the United States, there are about one and a half million blind people. That is less than one person out of a hundred. An even smaller number are born blind, like Sarah.

The fact that Sarah is totally blind means that she cannot see anything at all. But people may be "legally blind" although they can see a little. A legally blind person can see things no more clearly at 20 feet (6 m) than a person with normal sight at 200 feet (60 m). He or she cannot read anything smaller than the top line on an eye test chart.

A legally blind person cannot make much better use of his eyes than someone who is totally blind. For that reason, the law regards such people as being blind. They are entitled

to the same help in education, training, and getting a job that blind people are.

There are other problems with seeing that are much more common than blindness. Nearly half the people in the United States wear glasses. Some of these people are nearsighted. They can see things close up, but distant objects look blurred. Some are farsighted. They can see distant objects clearly, but the words in a book or magazine look like fuzzy, unreadable marks.

Yet with glasses, both nearsighted and farsighted people can see well. And there are other eye problems, some quite serious, that can be helped as well. To understand how, we have to find out something about the way the eye works. We have to take a look at how we see.

Light comes into our eyes through the *cornea.* The cornea is a transparent shell covering the central part of the eye. Like a window, it lets light in but keeps out dust and dirt.

From the cornea, light travels through the hole in a doughnut-shaped ring of muscle, the *iris.* The hole in the "doughnut" is what we call the *pupil.*

Being made of muscle, the iris is a most unusual "doughnut." It can swell or shrink in size. As it does, the pupil gets larger or smaller. In dim light, the iris opens the pupil wide to

A blind student studying for a math test. With his fingers, he is reading a math book printed in Braille. On the table in front of him is an abacus and a special Braille typewriter.

let as much light into the eye as possible. In bright light, the iris closes the pupil down to pinhole size. That keeps too much light from getting into the eye. All of this happens automatically, without your having to think about it.

You can watch the pupil change in size. If you go into a dimly lit room with a friend for a few moments, you will see each others' pupils get bigger. Step into a brighter room and they will shrink.

Just behind the pupil is the *lens.* The lens is made up of many very thick layers of protein tissue lying close together, like onion skins.

Light rays passing through the lens are bent. This forms a tiny upside-down image of whatever you are seeing. The lens projects this image onto the back of the eye.

The upside-down image at the back of the eye shines on the *retina.* The retina is a bundle of some 127 million nerve cells packed into a space about the size of a postage stamp. These nerve cells are sensitive to light. They react to the light of that tiny upside-down image by sending signals to the brain.

These signals are *nerve impulses.* Many nerve impulses can flow through a single nerve, one after another. They are a kind of code that tells the brain about the image on the retina. The impulses may be weak or strong. They may be spaced far apart or they may be bunched together. It all depends on what the image on the retina is like.

Bright light makes for stronger impulses, bunched more closely. Dim light makes for weaker impulses, spread more widely. Color, shape, and size also affect the code that flows from the eye to the brain. And it is in the brain that seeing begins.

This is not as mysterious as it sounds. If we really saw only with our retinas, we would see things upside down. For the image on the retina *is* upside-down. But we know from long experience that the floor and the ground are down and the sky and the ceiling are up. In our minds we have many clues to what is up and what is down.

But what happens if there aren't enough clues? Then we are not sure what we are seeing. For a while we see it one way, and then we see it another.

For example, which is the front end of the box on page 10, and which is the back end? The drawing doesn't have enough clues for us to be sure. As you look at it, the front and back ends keep changing places.

What's going on here? The drawing isn't really changing. Neither is the image of the drawing on the retina. We might say that we can't make up our minds about the shape of the box. It is in fact with our minds that we understand what our eyes are looking at. And that is what seeing is. Suppose the box is shaded to show which end is the front end. Now we see it one way, and one way only.

We can learn something else about the eye from that upside-down image. The lens of the eye is shaped like a magnifying glass and works in much the same way.

Hold a magnifying glass between a lighted lamp and a wall. The magnifying glass should only be a few inches from the wall. Now move the magnifying glass back and forth until you can see a clear upside-down image of the lamp on the wall. When the image is clearest, it is in focus.

Use a ruler, and measure how far the magnifier is from the wall when the image is in focus. Then try to focus the image of the lamp on a wall a few feet further from the lamp.

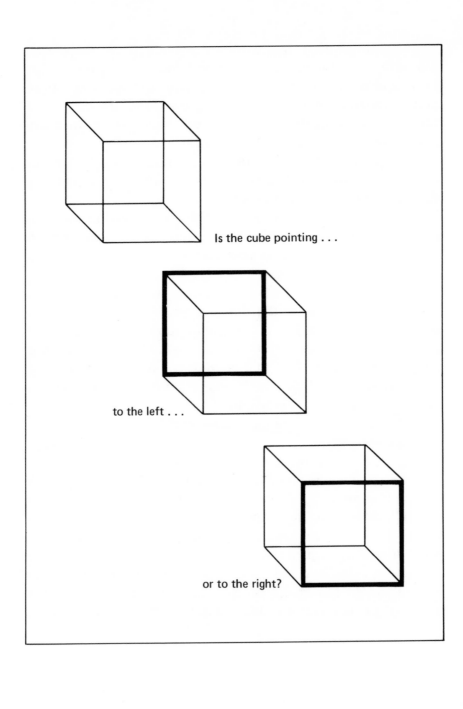

Is the cube pointing . . .

to the left . . .

or to the right?

What happens? You'll find that the magnifier has to be a little further from the wall to focus the image of a more distant object.

Your eyes have much the same problem. The lens of the eye projects an image onto your retina. For you to see clearly, that image must be in focus. But you can't focus on near and distant things at the same time.

If you hold your thumb about a foot from your eyes and look at it, things further away will look blurred. If you focus on things further away, your thumb looks blurred.

But how does your eye change its focus? After all, your lens can't slide back and forth like the magnifying glass.

You do it by changing the shape of the lens. Muscles at the edge of the lens suspend it at the front of the eyeball. When you look at something close, the muscles relax their pull on the lens. The lens gets thicker through its middle. The thicker lens can make a clear image of nearby objects on the retina. In the same way, you have to hold a thicker magnifying glass closer to the wall than a thinner one to make a clear image of an object.

When you look at things that are further away, the muscles cause the lens to stretch and get thinner. So in effect, you get two lenses for the price of one: one for near-seeing, and the other for far-seeing.

However, as people get older, the lens gets stiffer. Its shape can't be changed as much. The two lenses in effect become one. In nearsighted people, the lens works well for near vision, but distant objects are blurred. In farsighted people, the lens works well for distant scenes, but the print in a nearby book is blurred.

The lens does not usually become stiff until the age of 40 or so. But there are other things that can cause problems in

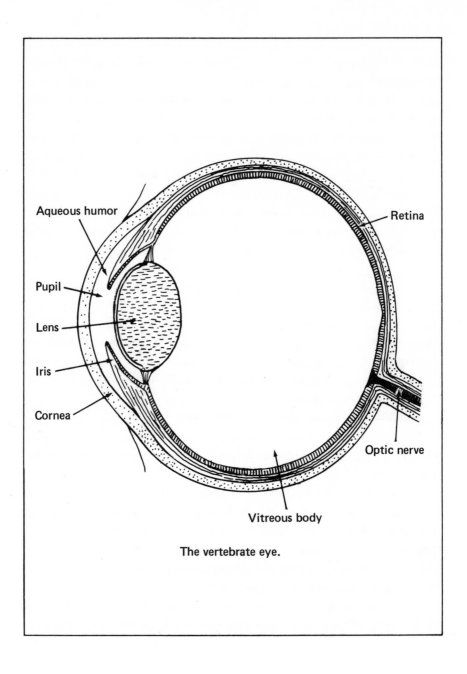

Aqueous humor

Pupil

Lens

Iris

Cornea

Retina

Optic nerve

Vitreous body

The vertebrate eye.

focusing at any age. The retina can be too near or too far from the lens for proper focus. The lens may curve differently in one direction than another. Then lines going in one direction will look clear while lines in other directions will be more or less blurred. This problem is called *astigmatism.*

Problems in focusing can almost always be cured by the right kind of eyeglasses. However, there are other problems that are harder to take care of.

Some of these are built into the way the eye has to work. The lens is made of living cells, much like the cells of the skin. These cells need food and oxygen. Skin cells get their food and oxygen from the capillaries—tiny blood vessels that branch everywhere through the skin.

The lens cannot have such blood vessels. If it did, they would block light from passing through the lens. Instead, the cells of the lens get food and oxygen from the fluids that bathe the lens. Between the cornea and the lens is a watery fluid called the *aqueous humor.* Between the lens and the retina is a slightly thicker fluid called the *vitreous humor.*

Like the cells of the skin, the lens cells grow old, die, and are replaced by new cells. Dead skin cells lie at the surface of the skin and simply flake and peel off. Dead lens cells cannot be shed that way. They would float in the eye, blocking vision.

What happens instead is that as new cells form and grow around the edge of the lens, the dead cells are slowly pushed into the center of the lens. These cells are still transparent. They do not twist and turn as they would if they were floating in the eye. So they do not interfere with seeing.

Sometimes, though, these cells break down and become cloudy, especially in older people. As the cloudiness increases, less and less light can get through the lens. Finally,

[13

the eye may become completely blind. Nobody knows exactly why this happens.

The cloudiness is called a *cataract.* Nowadays, when a person is becoming blind from cataracts, the clouded lenses can be removed. Soft plastic lenses can be put in their place. These lenses are carefully fitted to the curve and size of the eye. For that reason, cataract patients may see better with their new lenses than they did with their old ones—even before the cataracts.

Because of infection or injury, the cornea may also become cloudy. One way to restore sight is to remove the damaged cornea. Then an uninjured cornea is put in its place.

This new cornea comes from someone who has recently died. People may donate parts of their body to be used to help others after they die. They give permission for a doctor to take out a part of their body—a heart or a cornea for example—and give it to someone who needs it.

Replacing a damaged cornea with an uninjured one has saved the sight of many people. But there is sometimes a problem. Once in a while the new cornea may be infected with a virus, a problem that is difficult to detect before the cornea is put in.

If a patient receives an infected cornea, the infection will spread to his or her eyes. This can be very dangerous. A few patients have even died as a result of such infections. Where possible, eye doctors now use special drugs to help heal the injured cornea, instead of trying to replace it.

The fluids that fill the eyeball serve another purpose besides bringing food and oxygen to parts of the eye. They are under slightly higher pressure than the air around the eyeball. They help the eyeball to keep its round shape. Sometimes, however, the fluid pressure in the eye gradually becomes too high. This may happen because new fluid flows into the eye faster than the old fluid drains out of it, or for other reasons. If the trouble is not stopped, the increasing pressure gradually destroys the retina, causing blindness. This disease is called *glaucoma.*

Fortunately, an eye doctor can detect any change in eyeball pressure by a simple test, before glaucoma starts. In most cases, drugs can be used to reduce the pressure.

Cataracts and glaucoma are the two most frequent causes of blindness. Most cataracts can be treated, and glaucoma can usually be prevented. But once glaucoma has destroyed the retina, it cannot be restored or replaced. Blindness is permanent.

There are a number of other diseases besides glaucoma that affect the retina. Some damage only parts of it, causing poor vision rather than complete blindness. Some completely destroy the retina.

Many of these diseases cannot now be prevented or cured. Their victims are permanently blinded. But they can be helped in many ways. They can be helped by devices such as talking books or machines that can help them read with their fingertips. We'll see more about these in later chapters.

Chapter 3
SARAH AND MARGOT

Seeing is the most important of the five senses.

At least that's the way it seems to those of us who can see.

Our very habits of speech show how important we think seeing is. We say, "I see," when we mean, "I understand." When we don't understand, we're "in the dark." And when we remember something, no matter how complicated, we see it "in our mind's eye."

Well, why not? After all, a memory is a vivid picture in the mind, isn't it?

Think of last year's birthday party. Friends gathered around a table, a cake, lighted candles, voices singing "Happy Birthday" . . .

[17

Voices singing? That's not a sight, but a sound. Yet it's an important part of the memory, so important that we automatically think of it as a part of the picture in our mind. And there are many other parts of the memory that have nothing to do with seeing: the smell and taste of the cake, the rustle and feel of paper as gifts are unwrapped, and the laughter of our friends.

We "see" all that "in our mind's eye." The picture of the party in our memory is very different from a snapshot of the party taken by a camera. The snapshot only shows what can be seen. The memory shows the whole experience. And that's much more than mere seeing.

If we are blind, of course, seeing is not part of the memory at all. For people who can see, that is a very frightening thought. Again, the way we use words tells us a lot about how scary blindness seems to be.

A blind alley is a place with no way out. A blind rage is anger completely out of control. A blind panic is total unthinking fright. That pretty much reflects what we think it is like to be blind. It is hopeless, helpless and terrifying.

Being blind is being in the dark forever. That's what Margot thought when she met Sarah. The thought kept ringing through her head like a dismal chant.

Sarah was the only blind child in the class. The teacher had asked Margot to help Sarah learn where things were in the classroom. Sarah turned her head toward Margot and smiled when Margot introduced herself. But it was not the friendly smile that Margot noticed first.

A total lack of sight has not
stopped this boy from learning
how to play and enjoy the organ.

All she could see was that Sarah couldn't see. She's not *looking* at me, Margot thought. She's *listening* at me. She's turned her head toward my voice, and she's smiling at my voice. But her eyes are staring, and not at anything in particular. They're wrong-looking.

But Sarah was easy and interesting to talk to. In the first few days, Margot found it easier to talk to Sarah and listen to her without looking at her. She was fascinated at how important hearing and touching were to Sarah.

She thought for a while that Sarah must have really keen hearing and very sensitive fingers. Sarah kept telling her that wasn't true.

"My ears don't hear any more than your ears," Sarah said. "And my fingers aren't any more sensitive than yours. I just pay more attention to what I am hearing and feeling. I have to. But if *you* paid more attention, you'd find out that you're hearing and feeling the same things."

And Margot did. She learned to sit in her room with the door closed and the curtains drawn, listening to the picture her ears made of everything around her.

Behind her, the clock ticked on the mantel in the living room. To her left, tinny and hollow-sounding, an echoing ghost of her mother's voice floated through the air duct from the kitchen. Ahead and to her right, a cowbell tinkled. The sound came from the neighboring pasture. It grew fainter as the animal wandered away. The cow gets smaller and harder to see as it moves away, Margot thought. And the tinkling gets fainter and harder to hear at the same time.

The idea that touch was an important part of the picture in her mind was not as easy for Margot to accept. But one morning when she hopped out of bed, she discovered that her foot was asleep.

[20

Suddenly, Margot realized that it was awkward to walk with a foot so numb that there was little feeling in it. She had no idea where the foot was. She had to look to find out. Even when she looked, it still felt awkward.

She was used to knowing where the foot was, automatically, just by feel. Looking was no easy substitute for feeling.

Margot told Sarah about her discovery.

"It's as if there were a hole, an empty place in my experience, where that foot usually is," she said.

All that spring and summer, Margot got to like Sarah more and more. She'd almost forgotten how sorry she used to feel for Sarah, and how much Sarah had scared her at first. It wasn't Sarah that scared her, but her blindness, Margot now realized. It was almost as if blindness were catching.

Which it seemed to be, in a way. Margot didn't know exactly what had made Sarah blind, and she wasn't sure Sarah knew. But if it could happen to Sarah, it could happen to her. That was a frightening idea. Margot felt that if she were blind, she would be hopelessly lost.

Yet she no longer thought of Sarah as helpless. They shared so many things now: their love of music; books that had a good solid story to them; the long, slow walks through the pasture behind Sarah's house.

Yet sometimes, Margot had to help Sarah find her way in a strange place, and Sarah groped or stumbled over an unexpected obstacle. It was so unlike her sure easy pace through her home and around her neighborhood. It always brought back to Margot her first sight of Sarah and that dreary refrain: Being blind is being in the dark forever and ever.

It was funny how vividly she could hear it because she'd never spoken it, not out loud, and certainly not to Sarah.

Sarah had given her a lot—as much as she'd given to

Sarah. So many new ways of noticing things. Like that hot, still day they strolled past the pine trees on the edge of the pasture. A breeze had sprung up, blowing through the trees and cooling the girls.

"I like a wind through the pines on a hot day," Sarah said.

"A cool breeze, anyway," Margot agreed, "and this one sure is!"

"No, it's not. It's icy. It reminds me of winter."

"Oh, come on, Sar!"

"Listen! Listen to it, Margot."

Margot listened. She heard what Sarah meant. It was not like the rustling wind through the branches of a broad-leaved tree. It was a soft sighing sound with a faint hiss to it. It was like a high-pitched, feathery whistle from very far away —the sound of a wind hurrying snow before it. If she closed her eyes, she could almost see the snow . . .

Today had been a day like that one. Lying in the hot, close bedroom, Margot wished she could dream up some snow. But there was no wind to stir the curtains or bring any sound from the pines through the window.

Beside her, Sarah was sound asleep. The girls had spent the long August day playing together. After dinner, Sarah's parents had gone out. They wouldn't be back for hours. Sarah and Margot, who was staying overnight, had the house to themselves.

Margot wished she could sleep as soundly as Sarah. The night-light annoyed her. And it annoyed her that she still needed it, feeling she was really too old to need a night-light.

She was sleepy, but restless. The night-light doesn't bother Sarah, that's for sure, she thought. If I close my eyes, then I'll be blind like her and the light will go away. But it'll still be there if I want to open my eyes.

[22

Margot closed her eyes and made it dark.

She opened her eyes to the light; closed them—in the dark.

It was a kind of game, scaring herself and then proving there was nothing to be afraid of, and then scaring herself . . .

It was making her more and more sleepy.

Close. Open. Close.

Margot sat up in a panic. It was raining buckets and a cool wind was coming from somewhere. Where was she? She'd been dreaming something, but this wasn't her room and she couldn't see a thing.

Then she remembered. She was in Sarah's house. It was pitch black. Sarah was still asleep, and Margot didn't want to wake her.

But she wanted the light back on.

The night-light was on the wall near the window. Margot groped her way across the room. She strained her eyes, but there was nothing but a vague grayness. She let her hand walk along the baseboard until her fingers tripped over the light.

She grabbed it and turned the switch. No light. It was burned out, or the electricity was out. But she remembered seeing a flashlight on a little table at the end of the hall.

Margot turned her back to the breeze and aimed herself at the doorway. It was perhaps twelve steps to the door. On the second step her toes caught on something and down she went on one knee. Whatever she'd hit fell over with a clatter.

Margot sat still, almost holding her breath. Had she awakened Sarah? There was no sound but the rain. Then she heard the sudden flurry of movement and the sound of covers being tossed back.

"Margot? Margot? Are you there?"

She sounds almost as scared as I am, Margot thought.

"I'm here. The lights are out. A fuse must have blown. I'm trying to get that flashlight."

"Oh Margot. Stay there; I'll get it."

Sarah suddenly sounded very sure of herself again. Margot heard her get up, listened to the sound of her feet going down the hall.

Abruptly the night-light came back on.

Margot looked down the hall. Sarah was almost at the little table. Margot opened her mouth to tell her the light was on again, and stopped.

Silently she watched Sarah reach for the flashlight and turn back toward the bedroom.

Margot was quiet until Sarah reached the door. Then she said, "I'm here, Sarah."

Sarah walked over and handed her the flashlight.

"Thanks, Sar," Margot said. "You know," she added softly, "the light's back on."

"Why didn't you tell me then?" Sarah demanded.

"You were doing so well without it, Sar."

Sarah reached out for Margot's face.

"You're crying, Margot. I heard it in your voice. I'm glad . . ."

"Glad I'm crying?"

"No! Well, yes. Sort of. But that isn't what I mean. I mean I like to know what you're feeling, especially about me. Because I like you and I want you to like me.

"Sometimes, I think that's the hardest part of being blind. I can't see if somebody is smiling at me or frowning at me— or sticking their tongue out at me. I have to figure out how people feel by what they say and how they say it. Or I have to feel their feelings, the way I just felt your tears."

[24

"But you know how I feel about you, Sarah. We're friends."

"Oh, sure, but friends can change and feelings can change. My being blind used to scare you a lot of the time. It doesn't now, but sometimes, just for a minute, I think you get that feeling back."

"Maybe so, Sarah. Anyway, I know what you mean about not being able to see feelings. When I knocked over that table and woke you up, you sounded scared, but I wasn't sure because I couldn't see you. Then all of a sudden you didn't sound scared. Why?"

"I was only upset because I wasn't sure where I was for a minute. Unlike some people, I'm not afraid of the dark. But I couldn't hear the hall clock, just the rain. And that was scary. Then I heard your voice and I listened harder and I heard the clock. There it was, where it's always been, like a little arrow made of ticks and tocks, pointing down the hall."

"Unlike some people, Sarah, I'm not afraid of a little silence. But I strained and strained my eyes and it was so dark . . ."

"You strained your eyes . . ."

"And *you* strained your ears for the tick of that clock!"

Suddenly, they were both laughing.

[25

Chapter 4
ECHO PICTURES; FINGERTIP WORDS

Eyes straining to catch the faintest glimpse of light.

Ears alert for the softest whisper of sound.

In fact, hearing and seeing have much in common. The lamp lights the hall for Margot's eyes. The ticking clock points the way down the hall for Sarah.

For Margot, when the light goes out it is dark. The dark can be frightening. It is frightening because we cannot see clearly what lies around us.

Sarah does not experience darkness in that way. But for her, silence can be much like darkness. Without sound, she is without some of her best clues to what lies around her.

There are many clues in sound. Margot was not surprised that Sarah could find her way around her home almost as if she could see. She understood that Sarah had a kind of picture or map in her mind of places that she knew well.

In strange places, Sarah moved slowly and cautiously. Yet even there, she knew when a wall or a tree was ahead of her.

Sarah teased Margot by telling her she could hear walls and trees and other large objects. But as far as Margot was concerned, the real explanation was nearly as hard to believe as Sarah's teasing.

The metal plates on the heels of Sarah's shoes made a sharp, high-pitched noise when they struck the ground. Like ripples spreading over a pond, *sound waves* spread out through the air from the noise. They bounced off nearby objects and came back to Sarah's ears as echoes. That is what an echo is—a reflection of a sound.

Echoes are easy to hear when they bounce off a hard, smooth surface. Try talking into a large, empty coffee can, for instance. The strange "hollow" sound is due to the many echoes of your voice bouncing back and forth and overlapping inside the can. You get the same kinds of sound when you walk and talk in a large room with bare walls. The less furniture is in the room, the more "hollow" it sounds. A room like that not only looks empty, it sounds empty.

But wherever we are, there are echoes. There are echoes from our footsteps, from our voices, from other sounds

This blind student, with his instructor, is learning how to restring a baby grand piano at a school for the blind in New York City.

[28

around us. We don't usually hear the echoes as separate sounds. Instead, they give a sort of *feel* to all that we hear. There is the hollow feel of sounds in an empty room, where echoes race back and forth many times. There is the quiet, soft feel of sounds in a room with thick carpets and heavy curtains. There, echoes are swallowed up almost before they start. On a damp, still day in the open country, there is a feel of great space. Faint sounds and fainter echoes reach us from far off.

Sound waves travel at 1,100 feet (335 m) a second. Suppose you hear an echo from a wall one second after you make a sound. That means the *round trip* made by the sound and its echo takes a second. The time it takes the sound to reach the wall is half of that—one half of a second. In one half of a second the sound has traveled one half of 1,100 feet (335 m), or 550 feet (168 m). So the wall is 550 feet (168 m) away.

Actually, we can tell sound and echo apart when they come much closer together than that—less than 1/100th of a second. And echoes do not sound quite the same as the sound which causes them. For that reason we can tell them apart even when they are so close together that the original sound and the echo overlap. That means we can measure short distances by ear.

That is how Sarah can tell when she is getting close to a fairly large object, like a wall. Of course she doesn't measure how long it takes for the echo to come back to her and then work out the distance like a problem in a math book. She judges the distance automatically, from long experience. She doesn't think about *how* she is doing it.

The same thing happens when you judge a distance with your eyes. If you're throwing a ball to someone, you don't stop to figure out how far away he is. You judge the distance with

[30

the clues you get from your eyes. You judge how hard you have to throw to make the ball reach him. When your muscles are set and the ball is aimed, you throw.

All of that can happen in less than a second. You may make a mistake and not aim the ball right. Or you may not throw it hard enough. But the more you practice throwing, the more accurate you become.

We learn to understand what our senses tell us through using them. Blind people most often must use their senses of hearing and of touch to take the place of sight. Blind people do not hear more or feel more than sighted people. They have just learned to pay more attention to what we all can hear or feel.

There are inventions that help blind people to do this. They help blind people use their other senses to build up a clearer and sharper picture of what's around them. One of the oldest of these inventions is Braille writing.

Braille is named for Louis Braille, a French teacher of the blind who lived from 1809 to 1852. Braille himself lost his sight at the age of three. In 1829, he designed the Braille system of printing and writing for the blind.

Braille is a system of raised dots that stand for the letters and sounds of a language. The dots are "read" by touch. An experienced Braille reader can scan 2,000 to 2,500 dots a minute with his fingertips. That's about 100 words a minute.

Braille brought a wealth of reading to the fingertips of people who could not see. Many books and magazine articles have been translated into Braille. Though Braille was a wonderfully useful invention in its time, it is not much used today. Only about five percent of those who are blind or can't see well enough to read print use Braille regularly.

Why? There are many reasons. A book printed in Braille

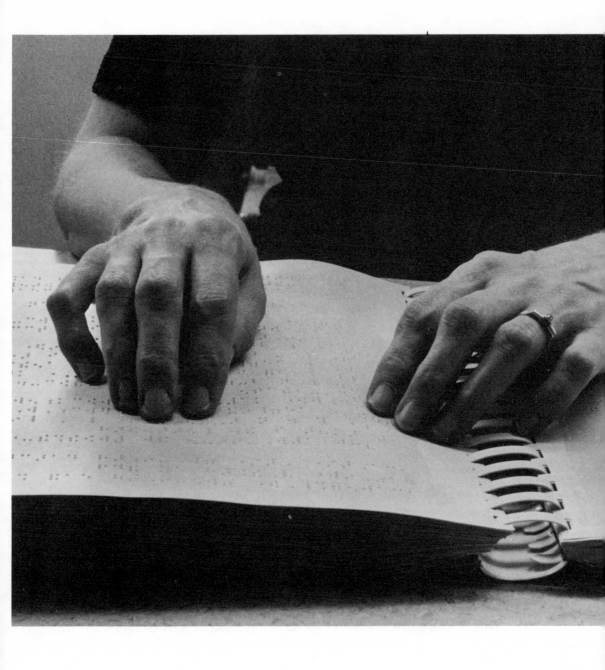

takes up a lot more pages than the same book printed in the ordinary way. Braille books are expensive, take up more library space than regular books, and are clumsy to use. As a result only about 350 of the 40,000 books printed each year are put into Braille.

It also takes a long time for a person to master Braille. Sometimes it takes many years for a person to learn Braille well.

But there is a happier reason why Braille is not used so much anymore. It is being replaced by newer inventions that are easier to use.

There are "talking books," for example. Merilyn Rosenthal is a blind student at Harvard Law School. Her study room is filled with stacks and stacks of "talking books"—tape recordings of law books, many of them over 900 pages long. Merilyn studies for lectures and exams by listening to her recordings. She borrows the tapes free from a national organization called Recordings for the Blind. Volunteers make the recordings by reading books for the organization.

However, tape recordings can also get to be bulky when you need a lot of them. And it takes quite some time for a volunteer to read a long book aloud. But in a few years, many blind readers will be able to read books in ordinary print as soon as they are published.

Braille is a system of raised dots that stand for the letters and sounds of a language. It is a system that enables blind people to "read" with their fingers.

One invention that will let them do this is the *Optacon.* It was invented by two scientists, Dr. James D. Bliss and Dr. John G. Linvill. Dr. Linvill's daughter, Candy, worked with her father and Dr. Bliss in designing the Optacon. Candy is blind.

One part of the Optacon is a hand-held camera, about the size of a small flashlight. The reader passes the camera over a line of print. Metal guide bars allow the reader to line up the camera with one row of print after another.

Almost like the human eye, light-sensitive strips in the Optacon camera scan the black-and-white print patterns. They translate these patterns into patterns of electrical currents.

The electrical patterns cause tiny pin-shaped metal strips to vibrate in the shapes of the letters the camera is scanning. The reader feels these vibrations with the tip of his or her index finger.

Candy has learned to be very adept at using the Optacon. Even so, reading with the device is slow. It is about half the speed of Braille reading. And Braille reading itself is half the speed at which a sighted person reads. Nevertheless, the Optacon makes it possible for a blind person to read anything that is printed.

Another device that lets blind people "read" was invented by Raymond Kurzweil, a student of computer science at a Massachusetts college. Kurzweil's machine can turn any book into a talking book. To be more accurate, the machine itself does the talking.

The hands of Karsten Ohnstad,
a blind author from Iowa.
Here he is writing in Braille,
with his stylus and guide.

The machine scans a line of print with a beam of light. Like the Optacon, it changes the print patterns into electrical patterns. But in this case, the electrical patterns are fed into a computer which is part of the machine.

The computer is programmed to translate the patterns into the sounds of the spoken language. In 1978, one of the first of these devices was set up in a public library in New York City. A blind man, Frank Perino, placed a copy of the poem "The Midnight Ride of Paul Revere" under the machine's glass cover. He pressed a button on the gadget's control board.

The machine beeped and began to "read" the poem. It did not always pronounce the words correctly, and it sounded, according to Mr. Perino, a bit like somebody with a strong foreign accent and a bad cold.

But that did not matter. If Mr. Perino did not understand a word, he could press a button and have the machine read it again. Or he could press another button to make the machine spell the word for him letter by letter.

(It's no wonder the machine doesn't always pronounce English correctly. Even *human beings* who learn English as a foreign language have a hard time remembering all the rules of pronunciation. In English, a group of letters like "ough" can stand for many different sounds. Try saying c*ough*, r*ough*, thr*ough*, b*ough*, d*ough*, for instance. Well, you *ough*t to get them right!)

With the aid of the Optacon,
a blind child can enjoy the
same books that youngsters
with normal vision can read.

Machines like Kurzweil's are not easy to obtain. In 1978, there were only 15 of them in existence, and they cost about $50,000 each. But as more and more of the machines are made, the inventor expects the price to go down to between $5,000 and $10,000. In the future, the machines will be cheap enough so that individuals, as well as libraries, can afford them.

There are also devices that help blind people get about more easily. In one way or another they do this by allowing blind people to make still better use of their senses, especially hearing. They send out sound signals or light beams that bounce off objects. The returning light beam or sound echo causes the devices to make musical sounds. The pitch and loudness of the tone tell the user in which direction obstacles are, and how far away they are.

Such devices are sometimes built into walking canes. But plain, old-fashioned walking canes are still used by most blind people. They are very helpful in strange surroundings. The cane itself can give warning of obstacles that lie ahead—a hole in the sidewalk, or the edge of a curb, for example. And echoes from the sharp tapping of the cane on the pavement give still more information.

Dog guides also can warn blind people of nearby obstacles. Most sighted people think of dog guides, or seeing-eye dogs, when they think of aids for the blind. But dog guides are used by only about five percent of the blind. Blind people who are used to traveling rely more on their own "obstacle

The Kurzweil Reading Machine translates lines of print into the sounds of the spoken language.

[39

sense." Changes in sound and echo tell them where obstacles are.

Some scientists are working on a device that may actually help the blind to see. The instrument depends on the fact that when any part of the visual center of the brain is stimulated, a person sees a flash of light.

Normally, of course, this happens when nerve impulses from the retina travel along the optic nerve to the visual center at the back of the brain. But it may also happen, for example, if a person is struck on the back of the head. He or she "sees stars." Blind people can see these light flashes, too. The flashes are called *phosphenes.*

If a point on the visual center of the brain is stimulated by a tiny electrical current, the person sees a phosphene. This tiny dot of light appears to have a definite position in space. Suppose another part of the visual center is stimulated. Another phosphene appears in a different position.

For each point on the visual center, a phosphene appears in a different position. A group of phosphenes can be made to form a *pattern* of light flashes. This is the idea behind creating artificial sight.

The basic instrument used is a miniature TV camera that forms an image of something. Each point of the image is turned into a very weak electrical signal. Each signal is sent to a different part of the visual center through very thin wires inserted directly into the brain. Since the brain itself cannot

With the aid of a dog guide, this young woman is able to get around the city campus of Columbia University School of Law.

[40

feel pain, the wires do not cause any discomfort. But the currents produce a pattern of phosphenes that reproduces the camera image. The user, therefore, sees this pattern.

So far, only very crude instruments of this type have been designed. They have been tried on a few blind volunteers. The volunteers were able to see simple patterns, including the shapes of letters.

All of these devices, as well as the reading devices, help blind people make do with the senses they have. They take signals that the blind cannot see and turn them into sounds they can hear. Or into vibrations they can feel, or phosphenes they can see.

In an important way, this is what all people do. They must use what senses they have. They must find their way around the limits of their senses. A poet or a storyteller may write about familiar things in a new way—in a way that has not been imagined before. A scientist finds ways to see the invisible, hear sounds beyond the reach of the ear, and weigh what is lighter than air.

In their power of imagination to break a path beyond what their senses tell them, blind people and sighted people are the same. They are people.

Chapter 5
OF BLINDNESS
AND A BUILDING

Sarah remembered her first meeting with Margot, and how nervous Margot had been. But then, everybody had been nervous. After she had been at school for a couple of weeks and knew her way around the building, the principal had called her into his office.

Mr. Auerbach chatted with Sarah about her school work. He told her he'd had good reports from her teacher. But he kept asking questions about whether she had trouble finding this classroom or that one. Did the stairs bother her? Did other kids dashing through the halls upset her?

Sarah tried to reassure the principal. He hardly seemed to listen.

Then the bell rang for the next class. Mr. Auerbach offered to walk Sarah back to her room. Sarah told him she knew her way. There was a pause. Sarah could tell from the way Mr. Auerbach was breathing that he'd started to say something once or twice and then stopped. Finally, he let her go.

Sarah turned right outside his door and headed for the stairway. Without thinking, she headed toward the stairs. She could hear voices, and the sound of shoes on the metal risers was right in front of her. She reached out, took the railing.

Up one flight. Down this hall. Right here, left there. And she was at her classroom door.

Oddly enough, Sarah thought that Mr. Auerbach was much less worried about her after that meeting.

She was right.

Mr. Auerbach had stared after Sarah as she left his office. She looked so sure of herself. Then he followed her, keeping seven or eight steps behind.

Kids walked or ran past her. Some said, "Hi," and she waved or nodded back. She kept going without a hitch, up the stairs and around the corners. He saw her walk into her room, turned, and went back downstairs.

Sarah was used to the idea that people who could see

Two students and their teacher, in a special school for the blind, using a relief model of the human digestive tract. Recent legislation will enable more blind students to go to school with their sighted peers.

were concerned about her. Whenever she met new people, she expected her arm to be grabbed so she could be guided to a seat. Or turned toward someone who was talking to her.

That wasn't the way she was treated at home. Yet even there, she knew, there had been a time when her mother and father watched over her anxiously.

Her parents had told her how afraid they had been that she might hurt herself. Even when she was in a playpen, her parents felt that one of them had to be in the same room with her.

As Sarah grew older, her parents didn't let her learn to feed herself. They still held the spoon and fed her themselves. They didn't like to let her play with other small children.

Sarah got restless and bored. "You *have* to let her learn to feed herself," a friend with a blind child told her parents one day. "Guide her hand for goodness sake! Do you think she's going to swallow the spoon? Let her walk. Let her jump. Let her have some adventures. Let her play with other children, and laugh and cry with them."

Sarah's parents tried. They taught Sarah to feed herself. They took her out of the playpen and let her explore the house. They let her play with other boys and girls.

Sarah enjoyed her new freedom. As time passed, she found other things to enjoy: the feel of cool grass on her bare feet; the smell of baking cookies; the contented purr of a cat.

Once Sarah asked her mother if cats purred with their tongues.

"No, I think they purr with their throats. What made you think they purr with their tongues?"

" 'Cause a cat's tongue feels the way a purr sounds— rough and raspy," Sarah answered. "What does it look like?"

[46

"It doesn't look nearly as interesting as it feels. Just little and red, Sarah."

"Well, I bet a purr doesn't look as interesting as it sounds, either!"

From that day, "purr" had a special meaning in Sarah's family. It meant anything that felt or sounded or tasted or smelled more interesting than it looked. Like a piece of sandpaper, or a misty rain, or an onion, or a drum.

When Sarah asked questions about how big she was, her dad built her a wooden archway in her playroom. When she stood under it she could just reach the top of the curve. The sides were just wide enough so she could touch them with her outstretched arms.

"Of course," her father told her, "that will change as you get bigger. You'll feel yourself getting too big for it."

Sarah liked the arch for other reasons, too. Outside, she told her father, it felt like the outside of a ball.

"It curves out like this," she said, shaping her hand. "But from inside the arch, it curves in like this. That must be the way a ball would curve if you could get inside it."

"You're right, Sarah," her father replied. "But I really never thought of a ball and an arch in just that way before."

Sarah's dad was pleased at her discovery. What it meant, he realized, was that she had an idea of how the shape of a ball might change when she "looked" at it from different points of view.

It was hard for him to think of words like "seeing" or "looking" in relation to Sarah. He shied away from such words. But in this case, Sarah certainly did have a picture, an image, in her mind. What is seeing anyway, he asked himself, if it is not to know the size and shape and position of something in the mind?

[47

In fact, scientists have recently discovered that even children who are born blind have ideas about the way an object's shape may seem to change from different points of view.

For example, you know that if you look straight down at a plate, it looks round. But if you look at it from the side, the plate looks like an oval instead of a circle.

A blind child pointing straight down at a plate will move his hand in a circle to describe the plate's shape. If he stands to one side and points to it, he moves his hand in an oval.

Scientists at the University of Toronto in Canada have worked with blind children for seven years. The children were first given pictures in Braille—pictures made of raised dots that they could feel with their fingertips.

They were given Braille pictures of the room they were playing in. There were several pictures of the room, each made from a different point of view. The blind children could tell almost at once where the picture was drawn from. They might say, "Oh, this was drawn from the doorway," or "That one was drawn from over near the window."

Sarah's father had read about such experiments. So he was not surprised that his daughter had a sense of the size and shape of things, and even of how they might appear from different points of view.

By the time Sarah was ready to go to school, much had changed between her and her parents. Of course, they knew that since she was blind there were things she couldn't do. But they thought first of what she *could* do, of her way with words and ideas and her eagerness to learn.

They knew that when Sarah grew up she would be living and working in a world full of sighted people. So they wanted her to go to public school where she would be playing and studying with all kinds of children. Years ago, Sarah would probably have been sent to a special school for the blind.

She would have lived away from home with other blind children. She would have been given special training in Braille. She would have learned how to take care of herself in spite of her blindness. For example, she would have learned how to label her clothes in Braille so that she would know what colors or style she was wearing.

Sarah would also have learned to avoid "blindisms." Blindisms are things like a shuffling, hesitant walk, or not turning toward someone who is speaking. This kind of behavior often makes sighted people very uncomfortable.

Most important of all, Sarah would have grown up and studied and learned surrounded by blind people. Her training and her experience would have been centered around just one thing—her blindness.

Now there are new laws about schooling for handicapped children. The laws say that these children must be allowed to go to regular public school where possible if their parents wish them to.

Some people don't think such laws will work very well. They say that the handicapped students will need too much attention from the teacher, and that they will distract the class and upset it. Under these conditions, nobody will learn much.

Some parents of handicapped children believe their children would learn better in special schools. They feel that few public school teachers have the training needed to teach handicapped children. They believe that people do not really want to accept handicapped children as they are. Letting them into public schools, they argue, is just a way of pretending that they are exactly like everyone else.

[49

There is some truth in these arguments. But there is also another side to consider. There are thousands of scientists and doctors in the United States who are handicapped, for example. Some are blind. Some are deaf. Some can't get about without a wheelchair. Yet they are doing difficult and important work. They are helping all of us, as well as themselves. Many of these professionals point out that they were very lucky to be able to get the training they needed. They had understanding parents who fought hard to get them into public schools. Special schools for the handicapped do not give early training in math and science.

There are certainly thousands of other handicapped adults who had talent, but who were not so lucky. They did not get the training that would have helped them become doctors or scientists. You could also say that even nonhandicapped people suffered from this. Society needs more well-trained people in science and the arts—not fewer.

It is true that students with certain kinds of handicaps might be distracting to a class. But in most cases, the class will not be distracted unless it wants to be. Handicapped students and students who are not handicapped can learn together. They can learn from each other, and from each other's needs.

*Blind persons can read about
nuclear energy and other highly
technical subjects from specially
produced booklets printed in Braille.
These booklets include raised
line diagrams that help explain
the scientific principles involved.*

This is what happened when Dr. Linvill worked on the Optacon. His blind daughter Candy worked with him and his colleague. Working together, they made a more useful machine than any of them working alone could have done.

The same sort of thing happens when an architect designs a building, such as a library, that can be used by the blind as well as the sighted. The architect adds guide rails along the walls for blind readers. He may use round studded rubber tiles on the floor that let blind people walk with more confidence and without fear of slipping. It also gives them a stronger feeling of where they are. They can feel changes in the slope or direction of the floor. The changes tell them they are at a particular place. So do dips and curves in the counters around the registration and card catalog areas.

And at the same time, these guides for the blind can be made attractive for sighted readers. The tiles can be colorful, the rails and counters graceful.

The whole spirit of such a building is the exact opposite of the special schools of past years. It does not ignore the handicapped. It says simply, Here is a place where people can learn together. Each may take from it what he or she needs.

Chapter 6
TO SEE BLIND PEOPLE

Today we have a number of laws to help people who are blind or handicapped in other ways. We have laws that are meant to give them an equal chance at a good education. We have laws to make sure that new public buildings will be easy for them to use.

These laws can help. It was not so long ago that most blind people grew up in a world separate from the rest of us. They went to special schools with other blind children. They were taught to do a few special tasks—the jobs that were "suitable" for blind people. They knew no other choices. So it is not surprising that most blind children in those times grew up thinking there was not much else they could do in the world.

Blind children's options were not so limited because their teachers did not care for them: It was because the teachers knew what the outside world was like. They knew that blind people were not considered fit for most useful work. In general, that was how sighted people felt about the blind. It was what they expected of blind people.

The special schools just reflected the way the outside world saw the blind. To the outside world, the most important thing about any group of blind people was their blindness. It was not that each person in the group might have a different talent. One might have musical skills, another might be good at mathematics, a third might write well. That was not considered important. What counted was that they were all *blind.*

Laws can give blind people a better chance to use their talents. So can some of the inventions of science. But neither can change feelings. Neither can change expectations. Unless we learn to see the blind as individuals, we will never appreciate their separate talents. And without appreciation, talents will not grow.

A blind person cannot see appreciation in a warm smile and bright eyes. But he or she can feel it in what we say and in how we say it, and especially, in what we do.

*Linda Webb, a blind typist
employed by IBM, uses a
special device to proofread
material she has typed. The
unit translates the letters she
has typed into the sounds of
English, enabling her to tell
by listening whether she has
made any errors.*

[55

Glossary

AQUEOUS HUMOR: The watery fluid that fills the space between the cornea and the lens of the eye.

ASTIGMATISM: In astigmatism, the lens of the eye is more curved in some directions than others. (See LENS; FOCUS). This causes objects to appear blurred in some directions. For example, the upright part of the letter "T" may look blurred while the line at the top is clear. Eye doctors test for astigmatism by having a person look at lines drawn in many different directions from a common center, like the spokes of a bicycle wheel. A person with astigmatism cannot see all the lines clearly at the same time. Astigmatism can be corrected by wearing the proper glasses.

[57

BRAILLE: A system of raised dots standing for the letters and sounds of a language. Braille writing is read by touch, passing the fingertips over the dots. It is named for its inventor, Louis Braille (1809–1852), a teacher of the blind, who was blind himself from the age of three.

CAPILLARIES: Very small blood vessels. The walls of capillaries are made up of a single layer of smooth flattened cells. Networks of capillaries spread through all the body's tissue. Food and oxygen pass through the capillary walls from the blood to the body cells. Carbon dioxide and other waste products pass from the body cells into the blood.

CATARACT: A disease of the lens of the eye. The cells of the lens break down, turning a cloudy milky white. As the cloudiness spreads through the lens, less and less light can pass through it. Total blindness may result. Cataracts can be cured by removing the clouded lens and replacing it with an artificial lens.

CORNEA: A transparent shell covering the central part of the eye. The cornea is in front of the iris and the lens.

ECHO: The reflection of a sound. Echoes are made when sound waves bounce off objects and are reflected back to you.

FOCUS: The point at which a lens forms a clear, sharp image.

GLAUCOMA: A disease of the eye caused by too much fluid pressure in the eyeball. If not treated, the pressure will injure and finally destroy the retina, causing blindness. Usually, medicines can be used to bring down the pressure.

IRIS: A doughnut-shaped ring of muscle behind the cornea. The hole in the "doughnut" is what we call the pupil. In bright light, the iris shrinks, making the pupil smaller

[58

so that too much light does not get to the retina. In dim light, the iris expands, making the pupil larger. In this way the eye can take advantage of what little light there is.

LENS: A curved piece of glass or other transparent material. All lenses bend light rays in some way, depending upon how the lens is curved. This bending changes the appearance and focus of things seen through the lens. Some lenses magnify. Others make objects look smaller. The lens of the eye forms a tiny upside-down image of whatever you are looking at. If the lens is working as it should, this image is in focus at the retina.

PUPIL: See IRIS.

RETINA: A bundle of some 127,000,000 light-sensitive cells at the back of the eye. Light from whatever you are looking at produces nerve impulses or signals in the retina. These impulses travel along the optic nerve to the seeing center in the brain.

VITREOUS HUMOR: A transparent, jelly-like fluid lying between the LENS and the RETINA.

For Further Reading

Davidson, Margaret. *Helen Keller.* New York: Hastings House, 1970.

Garfield, James B. *Follow My Leader.* New York: Viking Press, 1957.

Heide, Florence P. *Sound of Sunshine, Sound of Rain.* New York: Parents' Magazine Press, 1970.

Hunter, Edith. *Child of the Silent Night: The Story of Laura Bridgman.* New York: Dell, 1971.

Little, Jean. *From Anna.* New York: Harper & Row, 1973.

Weiss, Malcolm. *Seeing Through the Dark: Blind and Sighted— A Vision Shared.* New York: Harcourt Brace Jovanovich, 1976.

Index

About the Author

Malcolm E. Weiss was born in Philadelphia, Pennsylvania. He studied chemical engineering at the University of Wisconsin, English literature at the University of Chicago, and psychology at City College of New York. He worked for several years at Scholastic Magazines, Inc., where he became associate editor of *Science World.*

Since then, he has moved to Maine with his wife and two daughters, where he pursues a career in free-lance writing. The author of over ten books for young readers (including four award-winning science books), this is his first book for Franklin Watts.